THE ART OF PARENTING

SUN TZU'S THE ART OF WAR ADAPTED FOR PARENTHOOD

JOHN GRAFF

ELLIMAT BOOKS

For Elliott, my son.

The Art of Parenting: Sun Tzu's 'The Art of War' Adapted for Life's Greatest Battle - Raising a Child

Copyright © 2026 by John Graff

Published by Ellimat Books

Los Angeles, California

ellimatbooks.com

ISBN 979-8-9895666-5-5 (paperback)

ISBN 979-8-9895666-6-2 (e-book)

First edition 2026

Contents

Preface

I wrote The Art of Real Estate because I'd figured out, over a long career, that what Sun Tzu wrote for generals twenty-five hundred years ago applied to just about every serious human endeavor — negotiating, managing a team, trying to be first in a crowded field. That book found its readers. And once I started looking, I kept finding the same pattern everywhere.

Nothing tested the theory harder than having a kid.

Sun Tzu would probably hate the comparison, but it turns out he wrote one of the best parenting manuals ever — if you're willing to squint. Parenting, like war, is hugely important to the State, the State being your household at 6:47 on a Tuesday night. It runs on the same five factors. It's won by knowing yourself and your opponent — which here means knowing yourself and your kid. It's lost by long drawn-out sieges (mostly of bedroom doors), and by trying to reason with a small person who has stopped being reasonable.

What follows is a faithful adaptation — same shape, same voice, same thirteen chapters. Read a few pages at a time. The end of a long day is the right moment, ideally with something restorative nearby. If the gravity of the original feels out of place with sippy cups and sock refusals, I'll only ask: are you sure it is?

Some of this is a joke. Most of it is not.

John Graff

1

LAYING PLANS

Parenting matters enormously to a family.

It shapes character. It leads somewhere good or it doesn't. This is not a thing to wing.

Five factors run the show. Before you make any decision about your household, weigh all five.

They are: (1) Love; (2) Timing; (3) Environment; (4) The Parent; (5) Routine and Discipline.

Love makes the child want to go along with you — to cooperate even when it's inconvenient, even when the day is hard.

Timing is hunger and tiredness, mood and season. The hour before dinner. A long Sunday afternoon. The week of a stubborn cold.

Environment is where you are — home, large or small;

crowded or calm; open playgrounds or narrow grocery aisles. The odds of mischief, and of peace.

The Parent stands for wisdom, honesty, warmth, patience, and firmness.

Routine and Discipline means ordering the day into its parts, keeping the rules clear, making sure there's food and clothes, and managing what you spend.

Every parent should know these five. The one who does will raise her child well. The one who doesn't will struggle.

So when you're thinking about the state of your household, compare it on these points:

(1) Which household is full of love? (2) Which parent has more patience? (3) Who has timing and a calm home on their side? (4) Who holds routine more tightly? (5) Which parent is better rested? (6) Whose kids are more consistently guided? (7) In which household is praise and consequence more consistent?

Those seven tell me whether an evening will be peaceful or a war.

A parent who listens to me and acts on it will raise her kid well — trust her with the job. A parent who doesn't will face constant upheaval — hand her a coffee and listen sympathetically.

Take the rules, but take also any lucky break: the well-timed snack, the accidental nap, the grandparent who offers to take them for the afternoon.

When circumstances shift, shift your plans. The picnic rained out becomes a blanket fort in the living room.

All parenting is based on distraction.

When you mean to leave the park, appear to be lingering. When you mean to serve vegetables, serve them alongside something else. When you're in a hurry, don't act hurried. When you're exhausted, don't show it.

Hold out small incentives to get cooperation. Act surprised at their ideas, and they'll build on them.

If your child is in a good mood, enjoy it. If he's dug in, don't fight him — go around.

If your child is hot-tempered, don't match the heat. Play weak — can't open the jar, can't find the shoe — so he has to help.

If he's settled, leave him. If he's fixated, redirect without a frontal approach.

Move where he isn't expecting you. "Do you want to put your shoes on before your socks, or after?"

These little tricks work best when no one announces them.

The parent who wins bedtime has done the math in the kitchen beforehand. The parent who loses bedtime hasn't. Lots of planning leads to an early evening. Little planning leads to a late one. None at all, you can guess. That's how I can tell who will be reading in bed by nine, and who will still be negotiating at 10:30.

2

WAGING WAR

In parenting, when your household is one toddler, a baby, maybe a dog, and enough supplies for the week — between groceries and laundry, the cost of hosting visiting relatives, small expenses like wipes and batteries, and the shoes outgrown before they're worn — you'll go through more coffee than any reasonable person imagined.

When you engage in a real battle of wills, the longer it drags, the duller your patience gets and the weaker your conviction. Lay siege to a bedroom door and you'll wear yourself out.

If a standoff runs long, the evening doesn't have the resources to absorb it.

When your patience goes flat, your voice sharpens. When your energy is gone and you haven't yet opened the wine, other problems spring up to take advantage — the dog, the oven timer, the other kid. Then even the wisest parent can't prevent what follows.

We've heard of clumsy speed in parenting. We've never heard anyone call a forty-minute standoff over socks clever.

No household ever benefited from a long argument.

Only the parent who truly knows the cost of a long tantrum knows the value of ending one quickly.

A skilled parent doesn't repeat a command that failed, and doesn't threaten what she won't follow through on.

Bring the morning's energy with you, but also draw from the child's own enthusiasms. Then the afternoon has goodwill enough for its needs.

Low parental reserves mean the house runs on caffeine and short tempers. Short tempers at a distance deplete the kids too.

And an unoccupied child nearby means mischief rises; high mischief drains what peace is left.

When the peace is gone, the parents start bickering at night about small things.

With the peace drained and everyone exhausted, the house gets stripped bare — three-tenths of the living room given over to plastic and glitter; and replacement costs for lost lids, destroyed books, broken crayons, unmatched socks, and outgrown shoes will come to four-tenths of the month's budget.

So a smart parent leans on the child's own motivations. One hour of play he's chosen beats twenty hours of play you impose. One bite he picked beats twenty you had to coax in.

To get a child on your side, get him excited. For cooperation to feel worth it, he has to feel credited.

So when a small task gets done, thank whoever started it; name the specific effort. "You put your shoes on all by yourself." That's the right praise. And treat his contribution as your own work too.

This is using the child's interest to get what you need.

So in parenting, the goal is cooperation — not long arguments.

In the end, the parent is the arbiter of the household's mood. Whether the evening goes well or badly depends on you.

3

ATTACK BY STRATAGEM

The best outcome in parenting is willing, whole co-operation. Overpowering is a distant second. Better to have your child dress herself than to dress her; better to have her eat than to feed her; better for her to want to sleep than to be forced to bed.

Winning every small contest is not excellence. Excellence is avoiding the contest.

The highest form of parenting stops a tantrum before it starts. Next best is interrupting it before it gathers force. Next is managing it once it's going. And the worst possible move is reasoning with a three-year-old mid-meltdown.

The rule: don't reason with a child in a meltdown if you can possibly help it. Laying out arguments, citing prior agreements, appealing to fairness — that takes twenty minutes. Then stacking logic against feeling takes twenty more.

The parent, losing her grip on her own irritation, flings reasoning at the child like a swarm of bees. Her voice cracks. The child is untouched. This is what comes of a reasoned debate with a small person who has lost the ability to listen.

So a skillful parent quiets the tantrum without argument. Diverts the meltdown without reason. Ends the standoff without negotiation.

With her composure intact, she redirects the afternoon. And because she hasn't lost her temper, her authority is complete. This is winning by strategy.

The rule in parenting: two adults to one child, you can insist. Even match, negotiate. Outnumbered, divide them.

Equal stubbornness? Offer a choice. Short on patience that day? Retreat to a coloring book. Badly outmatched in energy? Put on a cartoon without apology.

A tired parent can make a stubborn stand, but she will lose to a four-year-old who has picked her hill.

The parent is the wall of the household. If the wall is solid, the household is strong. If it has gaps, the household is weak.

There are three ways a well-meaning adult brings trouble on a household:

(1) Issuing a command that can't be followed — "stop crying" — not realizing the child literally can't comply. That's useless instruction.

(2) Running the house the way you run the office, unaware that small children don't operate by office rules. This creates confusion.

(3) Handing out consequences inconsistently, not realizing that kids read patterns, not announcements. That shakes their faith in the world.

When a household is unsettled and distrustful, trouble comes from every direction. That's bringing chaos in and throwing peace out.

So there are five essentials for a good evening: (1) She wins who knows when to insist and when to let go. (2) She wins who can handle both the cooperative child and the defiant one. (3) She wins whose household runs on a shared spirit. (4) She wins who, being prepared herself, waits to meet the child at his most open. (5) She wins who is able to parent and isn't undermined by her partner.

As the saying goes: know the child and know yourself, and a hundred bedtimes hold no fear. Know yourself but not the child, and every good evening comes with a bad one. Know neither, and you'll struggle with everything.

4

TACTICAL DISPOSITIONS

G ood parents of old first made themselves hard to exhaust, and then waited for the right moment to meet their child.

Not getting exhausted is in your hands. Whether the child shows you an opening is up to the child.

So a good parent can secure herself against depletion, but can't guarantee the child's cooperation.

As the saying goes: you may know how to parent and still, in a given moment, be unable to do it.

Securing yourself against depletion is defense — sleep, food, a moment alone. Guiding the child is offense.

Playing defense means you're low on reserves. Going on offense means you have patience to spare.

The parent good at conservation hides in the deepest corner of the pantry. The one good at engagement springs out from the highest point of play. On one hand, preserving yourself; on the other, leading the day well.

Anyone can see a good evening once it's visible to the whole room. That isn't skill.

Nor is it skill if you win a loud argument and the whole extended family says, "Well done!"

Picking up a dropped toy is no sign of great strength. Noticing a full cup about to tip is no sign of sharp eyesight. Hearing a siren down the block is no sign of sharp ears.

A skilled parent is one who not only prevails, but prevails easily.

So her victories earn her neither a reputation for wisdom nor applause for forbearance.

She wins her evenings by making no avoidable mistakes. Making no avoidable mistakes is what guarantees a good night — it means she's guiding a child already inclined to be guided.

So a skilled parent puts herself in a position where breakdown is unlikely, and doesn't miss the moment when her child is open to her.

In parenting, the one destined to win only engages after

the ground is prepared. The one destined to lose engages first and then hopes.

A great parent grows love steadily and holds routine firmly. That's how she shapes the day.

The method, in order: first Observation; second Assessment; third Calculation; fourth Judgment; fifth Good Outcomes.

Observation comes from attention. Assessment from Observation. Calculation from Assessment. Judgment from Calculation. Good Outcomes from Judgment.

A well-fed, well-rested child up against a hungry and tired one is like a pound against a single grain.

The momentum of a cooperative child is like the burst of laughter at the first joke of the morning.

5

ENERGY

Caring for three children is the same as caring for one. It's only a matter of dividing your attention.

Parenting three in a car is no different from parenting one. It's only a matter of songs and hand signals.

Getting your household through a long day without breaking — that's a matter of alternating direct and indirect: a firm hand, then a playful nudge.

Making your authority feel unshakeable is the art of knowing exactly when to insist.

In all parenting, you use the direct approach to set clear rules. You use the indirect approach to get cooperation.

Indirect approaches, used well, are inexhaustible as earth and sky, endless as rivers. Like the songs and stories that have calmed children for a thousand years, they end only to begin again.

There are only five notes, but combined they make more lullabies than anyone could sing.

There are only a few snacks a kid reliably eats, but rotated they make more meals than anyone could eat.

There are only a few games in a small child's repertoire, but combined with imagination they fill more afternoons than you'll ever need.

In parenting there are only two approaches, direct and indirect, but together they produce an endless stream of strategies.

Direct and indirect flow into each other. Like a toddler circling a coffee table, you never reach the end. Who could exhaust the combinations?

A well-timed giggle is like a rushing current that even carries away the beginning of a tantrum.

A firm decision is like the sudden swoop of a falcon: the calm "no," spoken once.

So a good parent is decisive in her refusals and quick in her yeses.

Energy is the drawing of a bow. Decision is the release of the trigger.

Breakfast may look like total chaos and still have no real

chaos in it. Your morning may have no obvious structure and yet be impossible to defeat: the kids arrive at school on time.

Acting calm assumes real steadiness underneath. Acting patient assumes real love underneath. Acting cheerful assumes real reserves of strength.

Hiding your fatigue under a cheerful face is a discipline. Covering irritation with curiosity takes practice. Masking your agenda with the child's interests is done through suggestion.

A parent skilled at engagement keeps up the appearance the child will act on. She lets her own preferences go so the child feels chosen.

Holding out a story, she keeps him moving toward bed. Letting him lead, she brings him where he needs to go.

The clever parent pays attention to the combined mood of the household and doesn't demand too much on any given day. That's how she picks the right battles and uses collective energy.

When she conserves her energy, her children become like rolling stones. A tired child stops; a rested one keeps going. An overwhelmed one stalls; a child given space keeps rolling.

The energy of a well-parented child is like a round stone rolling down a grassy hill. So much for energy.

6

WEAK POINTS AND STRONG

Whoever is first to the bath, and waits calmly for bedtime, will come through the evening fresh. Whoever arrives second and has to rush will get there exhausted.

So the clever parent imposes her shape on the evening. She doesn't let the evening impose a shape on her.

Holding out a special story, she can make the child come to the bath willingly. Or, by threatening to lose the story, she makes delay unappealing.

If the child is relaxed, she can steer his energy toward tidying. If he's well-fed, she can ask him to wait a little. If he's absorbed in something, she can pull him away before he resists.

Show up at points the child has to defend — "Whose shoes are these in the middle of the floor?" — and move fast to places he doesn't expect you.

A parent can walk great distances through a day without strain, if she walks through territory with no conflict in it.

You're guaranteed to succeed at your requests if you only ask for things the child doesn't want to resist. Your household is safe if you only hold positions that can't be challenged.

So the skillful parent asks in ways the child doesn't know how to refuse, and refuses in ways the child doesn't know how to argue with.

O divine art of subtlety and secrecy! Through you, the vitamins are set out invisibly. The greens are folded into the pasta silently. And we hold the evening in our hands.

You can ask and meet no resistance if the timing is right. You can withdraw without protest if you move faster than the child can notice.

If we want to engage, the child can be drawn out even from behind a book and headphones. We only have to mention something she cares deeply about.

If we don't want to engage, we can keep the child from engaging us even if the coloring book is right there on the

What no one sees is the strategy that makes the easy evening possible.

Don't repeat the move that won you one good evening. Let your methods change as the circumstances change.

Parental tactics are like water. Water runs away from high ground and flows downhill.

So in parenting, avoid what's strong — the thing the child is firmly set on — and work through what's soft.

Water takes the shape of the ground it flows over. A parent takes the shape of the child she's raising.

Just as water has no constant shape, parenting has no constant conditions. What worked last month may not work today. What worked this morning may not work tonight.

A parent who can change her approach with her child and still raise him well can be called a natural.

The five elements of a parent's life — sleep, food, coffee, patience, love — are not always balanced the same way. The four seasons of a child's life — baby, toddler, school-child, teenager — take their turns. There are short naps and long ones. A parent waxes and wanes.

7

MANEUVERING

In parenting, the adult takes her orders from circumstance.

Having gathered her kids and concentrated her attention, she has to blend what's in front of her — the cranky and the cheerful, the hungry and the overfull, the eager and the reluctant — before setting up camp.

Then comes the actual work of moving through the day, and nothing is harder. The difficulty is in turning the long into the short, and the dull into the delightful.

Taking the winding route home after pulling the child from the playground gate, and reaching the bath before the other families even though you left after them — that's the art of redirection.

Maneuvering with one child is manageable. Maneuvering with three is dangerous.

If you load up a whole expedition to grab a short morning outing, you'll be too late. On the other hand, leaving without the diaper bag means sacrificing everything.

If you order your family to skip breakfast and tumble into the car without their shoes in order to get a head start, the leaders of your three divisions will fall to their own moods.

The calmer ones arrive first. The crankier ones fall behind. On this plan, only a tenth of the outing will actually be enjoyed.

Cut the morning routine in half to beat the clock, and you'll lose your oldest child's goodwill; only half your force arrives in decent shape.

Cut by a third with the same plan, and two-thirds arrive in decent shape.

So: a household without the diaper bag is lost; without snacks, lost; without the favorite stuffed animal, lost.

You can't ally with another family without knowing their rules — on screen time, on sugar, on the mood of their own small ruler.

You can't lead an outing without knowing the territory — the bathrooms, the benches, the steps, the dead-ends.

You can't turn a natural advantage into anything useful without local guides: other parents, the librarian, the grandmother who knows the shortcut.

In parenting, practice misdirection, and you'll succeed. "Shall we skip to the car, or hop to the car?" is a better question than "Shall we go to the car?"

Whether to focus on one child or split your attention among several depends on the circumstances.

Be quick as the wind — when a window of cooperation opens, take it. Be steady as the forest — when the child tests the rule, don't waver.

In correcting, be like fire: immediate and clear. In comforting, be immovable as a mountain: present, present, present.

Keep your plans dark as night, so you don't make a promise you can't keep. And when you move toward bed, fall like a thunderbolt — fast, decided, without hesitation.

When good things come, share them among the children without fanfare. When you win an advantage, share the credit.

Think before you promise.

She wins who has learned the art of redirection. That's the whole art of the daily march.

The old manual on household management says: on a busy morning, the spoken word doesn't carry far enough — hence hand signals and predictable routines. And ordinary instructions can't be heard clearly enough — hence songs, chants, and visual schedules.

Songs and chants, hand signals and schedules are all ways of focusing the eyes and ears of small people on one thing at a time.

The household then moves as one body. Neither can the brave wander off alone, nor the reluctant fall behind. That's the art of handling a group of small children.

In the long evening, use soft light and quiet voices. In the bright morning, use clear schedules and sunny songs. Moods can be shaped.

A whole household can be robbed of its spirit. A parent-in-chief can be robbed of her composure.

A child's spirit is sharpest in the morning. By midday it's fading. By evening his mind is bent on one last thing before bed.

So a clever parent proposes the hard thing when the child is sharp, and offers only quiet things when the child is tired. This is reading moods.

Disciplined and calm, wait for the child's own regulation to come back. This is holding yourself together.

Being near the goal while the child is still far from it; waiting at ease while he's struggling with a shoelace; being well-fed while he's about to melt down from hunger — this is conserving your strength.

Not commenting on an older child's new boundary; not correcting a small mistake that's already fixing itself — this is reading the situation.

Don't argue uphill against a child's feeling. Don't push back against a feeling that's already coming down.

Don't chase a child who's pretending to run. Don't scold a child whose temper is still hot.

Don't take the bait of a provocation. Don't interfere with a child who is coming to you to make up.

When you have the child cornered, leave an exit — a way for him to comply without losing face. Don't press a desperate small person too hard.

That is the art of parenting.

8

———— ◆ ————

Variation in Tactics

In parenting, the adult takes her orders from circumstance, gathers her household, and concentrates her attention.

In a crowded place, don't linger. In country where other families gather, join with your allies. Don't stay in dangerously isolated positions — a long afternoon with a cranky toddler and no backup. In hemmed-in situations — the grocery store at five o'clock — fall back on strategy. In desperate positions — the night of the stomach bug — you simply endure.

Some lessons can't be pushed today. Some requests can't be denied today. Some rules have to be held firmly, some battles avoided, some demands refused.

The parent who really understands the value of varying

tactics knows how to handle her household.

The parent who doesn't understand may know her child's temperament well and still be unable to act on it.

A student of parenting who hasn't mastered varying her plans — even if she knows the Five Foundations — won't make the best of her days.

So in a wise parent's thinking, advantage and disadvantage are always weighed together.

Temper your hopes for an easy morning this way, and you'll still accomplish the essentials.

And in the middle of trouble, stay ready to seize any advantage — a moment of laughter in the tears — and you can pull yourself out of it.

Ease a hostile mood by heading it off. Make space for the hostile feeling rather than argue with it. Hold out irresistible bait — "Shall we run to the car?" — and the children will rush where you want them.

The art of parenting teaches us not to rely on the hope that the child won't have a bad day, but on our own readiness to meet him. Not on the chance he won't melt down, but on the fact that we've prepared our position.

Five dangerous faults can undo a parent: (1) rigidity, which creates constant conflict; (2) timidity, which loses authority; (3) a hot temper, which any four-year-old can trigger; (4) sensitivity to other parents' stares, made worse in public; (5) over-indulgence, which makes the whole household miserable.

These are the five faults that wreck a household.

When an evening falls apart and its parent falls with it, the cause will be one of these five. Worth meditating on.

9

THE ARMY ON THE MARCH

Now we turn to observing the child and reading signs of trouble. Move quickly through moments of joy. Linger in the neighborhood of curiosity.

Camp in high places: the spot from which you can see both kids at once. Don't climb into arguments in order to win them. So much for household warfare.

After a hard transition, put some distance between you and the memory of it.

When a child is shifting from one activity to another, don't throw a new demand into the middle of it. Let him finish the transition, then make your request.

If you're in a hurry to move on, don't approach him near a toy he hasn't put down yet.

Position yourself higher than the child — emotionally calm, physically at his level but mentally above the moment — and facing the light. Don't argue from below your own center. So much for the river of feeling.

Crossing a crowded public place, your only concern should be getting through quickly, without delay.

If you have to handle a difficult moment in public, keep water and snacks close, and put your back to something solid — a wall, a friend, a quieter corner. So much for public operations.

On a calm, easy afternoon, pick an easily accessible spot with the child on your right and safety behind you, so the challenge is in front and support is behind. So much for the easy day.

These are the four useful branches of parental knowledge that let the wisest parents outlast four successive toddler sovereigns.

All children prefer high ground — adult attention — to low, and sunny moods to dark.

If you're careful with your small ones and ground yourself every day, the household stays free of every kind of disease, and that means peace.

When you come to a hill or a bank — a hard moment, a

rising mood — take the sunny side, the light answer, with your steadiness behind it. That way you help the child and use the advantages of the ground.

When heavy rain has been falling in the child's heart, and the feeling you want to cross is swollen and foaming, wait until it subsides.

Places with cliffs of feeling and tears running between; deep silences, tight moods, tangled thoughts, unspoken fears, crevasses of shame — approach all of these with care.

Stay away from such places with sharp words. Let the child approach them in his own time, with gentle attention.

If there's hilly country near your child's mood — hunger, tiredness, overstimulation, or an expectation that wasn't met — notice it and address it. Tantrums and tears hide in places like these.

When the child is close and quiet, he's drawing on the natural strength of his contentment.

When he keeps his distance and tries to provoke a reaction, he actually wants you to come near.

If he presents a problem that's easy to hear — a small complaint, a simple request — he's often putting out bait. The real need is underneath.

Moving around his playthings, repeatedly fetching un-related objects, means he's looking for something he can't name. A sudden demand for attention means hunger or tiredness is coming.

A child's voice rising in sharp tones means a feeling is ambushing him. Startled reactions, tears over something small, mean a larger feeling is beneath.

A tall column of protest is a big feeling advancing. A low but sustained protest is the approach of exhaustion. Protest branching in several directions — hungry, bored, hurt, angry, none of them for long — means something unnamed is at work. A few small complaints moving back and forth mean the child is just unsettled.

Humble words and busy preparations — "I'll just do this one last thing" — are signs he's about to break a rule. Loud words and an advancing stride are signs he's about to retreat from a position he can't hold.

When complaints come first and open on two fronts at once, he's gearing up for a larger argument.

Peace offers without follow-through mean a plot: an attempt to get an advantage without paying for it.

When there's running around and the children line up behind one plan, the critical moment has come.

One child advancing, another retreating — it's a setup. Sibling drama designed to pull you in.

When the kids lean on the table and droop, they're hungry.

If those sent to wash hands start splashing the walls, the bathroom is being neglected.

If the child sees an advantage and doesn't go after it, he's exhausted.

If the baby gathers all her toys in one spot, she's ready to play. If she crawls away from them, she's ready to sleep. Noise at bedtime means nervousness.

Quarrels among siblings mean the parent's authority is thin. Rules shifting day to day mean rebellion is coming. Parents angry with each other mean the kids are exhausted by the tension.

A child who offers to help with chores, asks what's for dinner, and makes his bed unasked — he wants something.

Siblings whispering in small knots or speaking in low voices mean a conspiracy — usually a reasonable one, often a pleasant surprise, but always worth noticing.

Too many rewards mean the parent has run out of resources. Too many punishments mean deep distress.

Starting with bluster and then backing off when the

child cries shows a total lack of intelligence.

A child coming toward you with compliments wants a truce, and usually a cookie.

If the children's moods stay opposed for a long time without resolving or cooling, the situation calls for great watchfulness and caution.

If your patience is only barely equal to the child's need, that's still enough. It just means you can't make a direct correction. Concentrate what you have, watch closely, and call for reinforcements.

A parent who doesn't think ahead and makes light of her child's inner life will be captured by it.

If a child is corrected before he's formed an attachment, he won't submit. And without submission, he can't really be taught. If consequences aren't enforced after attachment has formed, he still won't be manageable.

So children must first be treated with warmth, and then guided by gentle firmness. This is a sure road to peace.

If daily rules are consistently kept, the household will be well-disciplined. If not, its discipline will be poor.

If a parent shows confidence in her child but still insists on her rules, both of them benefit.

10

TERRAIN

There are six kinds of parental terrain: (1) open; (2) entangling; (3) temporizing; (4) narrow pass; (5) precipitous heights; (6) distant.

Situations both parent and child can move freely in are open terrain.

In open terrain, be first to set the rule and carefully guard your line of patience. Then you can parent with an edge.

A situation you can enter but can't easily exit is entangling terrain: a promise too quickly given, a playdate extended on the fly, an activity started with no clear end.

From such a position, if the child is unprepared, you can sally forth and conclude it. If he's prepared for you and you fail to close it out, return is impossible and disaster follows.

When neither insisting nor indulging will work, the terrain is temporizing ground: the middle of the grocery store aisle.

Even if the child offers attractive bait for an argument here, don't stir. Move on instead, and pull the child after you. Then, in a quieter moment, you can address the matter with an edge.

Narrow passes — the car seat, the bathtub, the high chair — if you can occupy them first, hold them strongly and wait for the next transition to come to you.

If the child gets there first and makes the transition difficult, don't pursue while the resistance is full. Only pursue once it's thinning.

Precipitous heights — the edge of a meltdown, the point of no return — if you're there before your child, lower your voice and slow your pace, and wait for him to come up.

If he has reached them before you, don't follow. Retreat and try to draw him away with a different kind of attention.

If you're at a great emotional distance from your child and the intensity of feeling is equal, reconnecting isn't easy, and engaging directly will hurt you.

These six are the principles of the Earth of parenting. The adult with a responsible post has to study them carefully.

A household is exposed to six disasters that don't come from the child but from faults the parent is responsible for: (1) flight, the avoidance of the hard conversation; (2) insubordination, rules without warmth; (3) collapse, warmth without rules; (4) ruin, overreaction; (5) disorganization, inconsistency; (6) rout, loss of temper.

All else being equal, if one adult is thrown against three small children with no support, the result is flight.

When the children's demands are too strong and the parent's limits too weak, you get insubordination. When the parent's demands are too strong and the child too small to meet them, you get collapse.

When an older sibling is angry and untended, and takes it out on a younger one before the parent can figure out whether she can intervene, the result is ruin — not of the child, but of the afternoon.

When a parent is uncertain and has no authority; when her instructions aren't clear and sharp; when there are no fixed rhythms and the hours are a messy patchwork, the result is total disorganization.

When a parent can't read the child's state, and lets a tired one try a hard task, or pits a hungry sibling against a patient one, and forgets to put a snack in the front rank, the result is rout.

These are six ways to bring on a hard day, and the parent in charge has to watch for all of them.

The child's natural temperament is the parent's best ally. But the ability to read his mood, to control the forces of the afternoon, and to shrewdly calculate hungers, distances, and difficulties — that's what separates a great parent from the rest.

A parent who knows these things and puts what she knows into practice will parent well. One who doesn't know them and doesn't practice them will be defeated by a Tuesday.

If patience will bring cooperation, wait, even if your partner urges you to speak. If insisting won't bring cooperation, don't insist, even if your partner urges you to.

The parent who acts without chasing praise, holds her line without fearing disapproval, whose only thought is the child's well-being, is the jewel of the household.

Treat your children as your own heart and they'll follow you into the deepest feelings. Look on them as your own beloved young and they'll stay with you even through the long night of a fever.

But if you're indulgent and can't make your authority felt; kind-hearted but can't enforce your limits; unable to settle their disputes — your children become like spoiled travelers. They're no good to themselves and no good to the household.

If we know we're ready to engage but don't know that the child isn't, we've gone only halfway toward a good evening.

If we know the child is open but don't know that we aren't ready ourselves, we've gone only halfway.

If we know the child is open and we know we're ready, but don't realize that the hour, the place, or the company makes connection impossible — we've still gone only halfway.

So the experienced parent, once moving, is never confused. Once she has broken into the day, she's never at a loss.

As the saying goes: know your child and know yourself, and your evening won't be in doubt. Know your home and know your hour, and you can make the day complete.

11

THE NINE SITUATIONS

The art of parenting recognizes nine kinds of ground: (1) home; (2) the familiar outing; (3) the contested toy; (4) the open park; (5) the house of many cousins; (6) the long day out; (7) the difficult errand; (8) the hemmed-in car seat; (9) the moment of true desperation.

When a parent is fighting at home, it's scattered ground: the child has many refuges, and the parent has many distractions.

When she has ventured out on a familiar outing, no great distance from home, it's easy ground.

A possession each child imagines brings great advantage — a stick, a sticker, the window seat — is contested ground.

A place where both parent and child can move freely,

like the park or the backyard, is open ground.

A gathering that brings three or four households together, like a family holiday, is ground of intersecting allegiances.

When a parent has pushed into the heart of a long day, leaving a trail of snack wrappers and small grievances behind, it's serious ground.

Busy places — crowded museums, rugged trails, the party of a friend of a friend — are difficult ground.

A situation reached by one narrow argument and only escapable by winding negotiation, like the midnight bedtime standoff, is hemmed-in ground.

A moment in which the household can only be saved by immediate action — the child darting toward the street — is desperate ground.

So on home ground, pick your battles carefully. On familiar ground, don't linger in conflict. On contested ground, don't engage; redirect.

On open ground, don't try to block the child's way. On the ground of many cousins, link up with your allies — the other parents — and trust the shared rules.

On serious ground, stock up: snacks, patience, one quiet corner. On difficult ground, keep moving steadily.

On hemmed-in ground, use strategy — the absurd joke, the unexpected silliness. On desperate ground, act.

The skilled parents of old knew how to drive a wedge between the child's protest and his desire; to keep an older child's argument from feeding off a younger one's echo; to stop the good moods from being spoiled by a bad one, the reasonable siblings from being swept into the drama.

When the children's grievances joined up, they gently split them.

When it was to their advantage, they moved forward. When it wasn't, they stayed still.

Asked how to handle a full-blown, terrifying tantrum that's still growing, I'd say: start by naming the feeling your small opponent is holding onto. Then he becomes touchable.

Calm is the essence of parenting. Take advantage of the child's unreadiness to escalate. Move by unexpected routes — a hug, a whisper, a window opened — and address the feelings he isn't guarding.

Here are the rules for a parent leaving the house: the farther you go from home, the more unified your children become, and ordinary arguments don't survive.

Make forays into grocery stores and playgrounds to keep

the household supplied with variety.

Watch your children's well-being carefully. Don't over-tax them. Concentrate your energy, hoard your strength. Keep the day moving. Cook up unreadable plans: a sudden picnic, a bath with glow sticks.

Put your children in positions of small risk — the tall slide, the hard puzzle, the first sleepover — and they'll pre-fer courage to retreat. If they'll face the small fear, there's nothing they can't become.

Children in the grip of a big feeling lose track of time. If there's no refuge, they'll reach for you. In unfamiliar country they'll hold your hand. When there's no help for it, they'll fall asleep.

So without being lined up, the children will constant-ly watch you. Without being asked, they'll follow your mood. Without explicit orders, they can be trusted to try.

Don't read omens in one bad morning. Throw out the superstition that it's always like this. Then, until night itself comes, there's nothing to fear.

If our children aren't buried in toys, it's not because we're against riches. If their lives aren't overscheduled, it's not because we don't want to give them the best.

On the day they're sent off to school for the first time,

your children may weep, the ones clinging to your leg soaking your trousers, the ones looking back letting the tears run down their cheeks. But once they're brought to the classroom door, they'll show the courage of small heroes.

The skilled parent is like the shuai-jan snake, found in the Ch'ung mountains. Strike its head and you're attacked by its tail. Strike its tail and you're attacked by its head. Strike its middle and you're attacked by both at once. So with a household: address one child's feeling and another erupts. Address the second and the first finds a new grievance. Address both and the baby wakes up.

Asked whether a household can be made to act as one, I'd say yes. The siblings of Wu and the siblings of Yueh are rivals. But if they're crossing a river in the same boat and get caught in a storm — the thunderstorm on a camping trip, the flu sweeping through all three — they'll help each other the way the left hand helps the right.

So it isn't enough to trust in locked cabinets and cookies hidden on the high shelf.

The way to manage a household is to set one standard of kindness that everyone has to reach.

Handling both the easy child and the hard one well —

that's a question of using the ground right.

So the skilled parent moves her household as if leading a single small person, willy-nilly, by the hand.

It's a parent's job to be quiet and steady, upright and fair, to keep the trust.

She has to mystify her children with small surprises, keeping them in pleasant suspense. Pancakes or eggs? The park or the library?

By changing her plans and arrangements, she keeps the day from going stale. By shifting her attention and taking circuitous routes, she keeps them from fixating on what they can't have.

At the critical moment, the parent of a household acts like someone who has climbed a height and then kicked the ladder away. She commits to the bedtime, the goodbye, the appointment, and doesn't look back.

She closes the app and puts the phone away. Like a shepherd moving a flock, she guides her children this way and that, and no one asks where they're going, only trusting that the grown-up knows.

Gathering her household and bringing it through the day — this is the work of a parent.

The different approaches suited to the nine kinds of

ground; the choice between flexibility and firmness; and the basic laws of human nature — that small people aren't small adults, and that their reason runs on a different clock — these things must be studied.

When entering a hard day, the general rule is that going in deep brings cohesion; going in only a little way means dispersion. The home day gone sideways is often worse than the long drive taken together.

When you leave your own country — the familiar house — and take your family across unfamiliar territory, you're on critical ground. When other families and their children are on all four sides, the ground is intersecting allegiances.

When you go deep into a day, it's serious ground. When you've only been out a short while, it's easy ground.

When others' expectations press on you from behind and narrow time pinches in front, it's hemmed-in ground. When there's no refuge at all — the delayed flight, the bathtub with a screaming toddler and no towel in reach — it's desperate ground.

So on home ground, I would inspire my children with shared purpose. On familiar ground, I'd make sure my attention and theirs are closely linked.

On contested ground, I'd hurry past.

On open ground, I'd watch the perimeter. On ground of intersecting allegiances, I'd firm up my alliances with the other parents.

On serious ground, I'd ensure a steady stream of snacks. On difficult ground, I'd keep pushing down the road.

On hemmed-in ground, I'd block any escalation. On desperate ground, I'd remind myself of the absurdity of taking it personally.

A child's nature is to resist obstinately when cornered, to fight hard when he can't help himself, and to obey promptly when he's fallen into your arms.

We can't ally with neighboring parents until we know their plans. We can't lead an outing without knowing the land, its bathrooms and benches, its steps and slopes. We can't use natural advantages without local guides.

To be ignorant of any of these doesn't suit a thoughtful parent.

When a thoughtful parent faces a powerful mood, her skill shows in preventing the child's grievances from concentrating. She overawes the rising feeling, and its allies — hunger, tiredness, a cousin's teasing — are kept from joining in against her.

So she doesn't argue with every small complaint, and she

doesn't foster the power of others' opinions in her household. She carries out her own quiet plans, keeping the day's chaos in check. That's how she can turn mornings around and redeem afternoons.

Hand out small praises without regard to rule, issue gentle requests without regard to formality, and you can handle a whole household as if you had only one child to handle.

Confront your children with the act itself. Never let them see your design. When the outlook is bright, show them. Say nothing when it's gloomy.

Put your patience in real peril and it will survive. Plunge your household into small adversity and it will come out stronger.

It's precisely when a parent has fallen into harm's way that she can strike a blow for grace.

Success in parenting comes from carefully accommodating yourself to the child's purpose.

By hanging near his orbit, we'll eventually get to know the commander-in-chief of his feelings.

This is getting something done by sheer attention.

On the day you take up your command — the morning you become a parent — block the passes of certainty, destroy the records of how it was supposed to go, and stop the flow of comparison.

Be firm in the council chamber of your own heart, so you can control the situation.

If the child leaves a door open, rush in.

Get ahead of your small opponent by taking hold of what he cares about, and quietly time his arrival at the ground of cooperation.

Walk in the path of the rule, and adjust to the child until you can have the decisive conversation.

At first, show the shyness of someone being courted, until the child opens up. Then move like a running hare, and his resistance won't catch you.

12

THE ATTACK BY FIRE

There are five ways to parent with drama. First, the grand surprise. Second, the sudden silliness. Third, the unexpected outing. Fourth, total attention. Fifth, the direct and serious word, spoken softly.

To carry out a dramatic intervention, you have to have means available. Your capacity for delight should always be kept ready.

There's a right season for these interventions, and specific hours for starting a conflagration of joy.

The right season is when the mood is very dry. The special hours are when the afternoon has gone flat, when long rain has kept them inside, when sibling tension has built up without release.

When parenting with drama, be ready for five possible

developments:

(1) When a giggle breaks out in the household, respond with more of the same.

(2) If there's a burst of silliness but the children stay sullen, wait. Don't push.

(3) When the joke has peaked, follow with an invitation — "Who wants to help me make cookies?" — if it's doable. If not, stay where you are.

(4) If you can redirect from outside — a walk, a change of room — don't wait for the mood to break inside. Deliver the change at a good moment.

(5) When you start a dance party, be upwind of it. Don't try drama from a position of depletion.

Joy that rises in the morning lasts. A joke forced in a tired evening dies quickly.

In every household, the five developments of drama have to be known, moods tracked, and the right hours watched for.

Those who use joy as an aid to parenting show intelligence. Those who use quiet show strength.

Quiet can settle a household, but it can't heal everything.

Sad is the fate of the parent who tries to parent well

through hard moments without cultivating the spirit of play. The result is wasted time and general stagnation.

As the saying goes: the enlightened parent prepares her mornings well in advance. The good parent cultivates her patience.

Don't move unless you see an advantage. Don't engage your children unless there's something to gain. Don't argue unless the position is critical.

No parent should enter a fight with her child just to vent her own frustration. No mother or father should push a point out of pride.

If it's to your advantage, move forward. If not, stay where you are.

Anger can turn into laughter. Frustration can turn into contentment, often by dinnertime.

But words said in anger can't be unsaid. A child's trust, once broken, can only be slowly rebuilt.

So the enlightened parent is watchful. The good parent is careful. That's how you keep a household at peace and a child's heart intact.

13

THE USE OF SPIES

Raising a child for even six short years costs a parent a lot and drains the household. The daily expense will be more coffee than you could have imagined. There will be commotion at home and abroad, and adults will collapse exhausted on the couch. Seven hundred loads of laundry will pile up waiting to be folded.

Parent and child may face each other for years, working toward the harmony that gets established over a single decade. Given that, staying ignorant of the child's inner life just because you don't want to do the work of careful inquiry is foolish.

A parent who does that is no guide to her child, no help to her household, no master of the art.

What lets a wise parent and a good partner understand

and act — and achieve things beyond what ordinary adults can — is foreknowledge.

This foreknowledge can't be pulled from books alone. It can't be drawn inductively from your own childhood, or deduced from general principles.

The child's dispositions can only be known from many sources.

So we use informants. There are five kinds: (1) teachers; (2) pediatricians; (3) other parents; (4) siblings and cousins; (5) the child himself.

When all five are at work, no secret of the child is hidden. This is called the fine web of attention. It is the parent's most precious faculty.

Having teachers as informants means attending closely to what they see: the child in company, the child frustrated, the child without you.

Having pediatricians as informants means listening carefully to what the body tells, even when the child can't.

Having other parents as informants means making friends with parents whose children are a little older — who've already walked the road you're on.

Having siblings and cousins as informants means noticing what they say when no adult seems to be listening, and noticing what they don't say.

Having the child himself as an informant means, over years, building the conditions in which he'll tell you the truth.

No one in the household should be more closely connected to than the child himself. No one should be more generously received. No other work demands as much patience.

A parent can't really be informed without intuitive attention.

She can't run her household without warmth and honesty.

Without some subtle ingenuity of mind, you can't make certain of the truth of children's reports, because children, like all reporters, are partial, imaginative, and sincere.

Pay attention. Pay attention. Use your sources in every kind of situation.

If a parent divulges a confidence before the time is ripe, the child's trust is damaged. Keep the confidence.

Whether the goal is to comfort a fear, manage a friendship, or understand a withdrawal, you always have to start by finding out the small facts: the names of the kids in the class, the shape of the playground, the songs at circle time.

Our attention has to gather these.

The child's reports that come to you unprompted should be welcomed warmly, met with interest, and neither corrected nor overmined. That way he keeps telling you what he sees.

It's through the information the child brings himself that we understand the teacher's remark, the friend's mother's raised eyebrow, the sibling's sigh.

It's because of his openness that we can address, with grace, the small sorrows and large fears we couldn't have known otherwise.

And in the end, it's by his report that our long work as parents can be adjusted to the true shape of his life.

The point of attention in all five forms is knowledge of the child. And that knowledge can only come, in the first instance, from the child himself. So he has to be treated with the utmost regard.

In the old days, the rise of a good household wasn't due to grand schemes but to quiet counsel, faithfully kept. The flourishing of a family depends, likewise, on the small words of small people, whose reports, rightly attended, are precious beyond measure.

So only the enlightened parent and the wise partner will

use the highest attention of the household to know the child — and by doing so achieve great results. Attention is the single most important element in parenting. On it depends a family's ability to move together.

THE END.